Oh My
Baby Boy

James Jaskolski

AuthorHouse™
1663 Liberty Drive
Bloomington, IN 47403
www.authorhouse.com
Phone: 833-262-8899

Interior Image Credit: James Jaskolski

This book is printed on acid-free paper.

ISBN: 978-1-6655-7141-8 (sc)
ISBN: 978-1-6655-7143-2 (hc)
ISBN: 978-1-6655-7142-5 (e)

Print information available on the last page.

Published by AuthorHouse 10/05/2022

author**HOUSE**®

By Jamie Jaskolski

To Luca

Follow
Your
Dreams

I'll love you for all
of my Years

I'll take away all
of your fears

And Oh My Baby Boy

I'll love you
with all that I have

And Oh My
Baby Boy

with every second
of every minute

And every hour
of every day

Through all the years
filled with joy

Oh how I'll Love you,
my sweet Baby Boy

The End

Printed in the United States
by Baker & Taylor Publisher Services